URSA MAJOR

The Myth and Science of Astronomy

Simon Rose

LIGHTBOX
openlightbox.com

LIGHTBOX

Go to **www.openlightbox.com**, and enter this book's unique code.

ACCESS CODE

LBS 59869

Lightbox is an all-inclusive digital solution for the teaching and learning of curriculum topics in an original, groundbreaking way. Lightbox is based on National Curriculum Standards.

STANDARD FEATURES OF LIGHTBOX

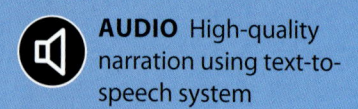

AUDIO High-quality narration using text-to-speech system

ACTIVITIES Printable PDFs that can be emailed and graded

SLIDESHOWS Pictorial overviews of key concepts

VIDEOS Embedded high-definition video clips

WEBLINKS Curated links to external, child-safe resources

TRANSPARENCIES Step-by-step layering of maps, diagrams, charts, and timelines

INTERACTIVE MAPS Interactive maps and aerial satellite imagery

QUIZZES Ten multiple choice questions that are automatically graded and emailed for teacher assessment

KEY WORDS Matching key concepts to their definitions

Copyright © 2016 Smartbook Media Inc. All rights reserved.

2 *Ursa Major*

Contents

Lightbox Access Code 2

Studying the Night Sky 4

Storytelling 6

Ursa Major the Great Bear 8

The Origins of Ursa Major 10

Astronomy through History 12

Ursa Major over Time 14

Mapping Planetariums 16

Careers in Astronomy 18

Sky Facts 19

Astronomy Q and A 20

Create Your Own Star Catalog 21

Know Your Stars Quiz 22

Key Words/Index 23

Log on to www.openlightbox.com 24

The Myth and Science of Astronomy

Studying the Night Sky

The study of stars and other objects in space is called astronomy. Groups of stars that form patterns in the night sky are known as constellations. They appear in different parts of the sky at different times of year. There are also some constellations that can be seen only from the Northern or the Southern **Hemisphere**. A star chart, or map of the sky, helps sky watchers find constellations.

Civilizations in the Middle East began naming stars and constellations thousands of years ago. About the same time, people named the signs of the zodiac. The zodiac is an imaginary band in the sky divided into 12 constellations that represent characters and animals. The first **telescopes** were used to study the stars in the early 17th century. Today, scientists called astronomers use large, powerful telescopes to observe **comets**, **galaxies**, stars, and planets. Planets are large objects in space that travel around a star, such as Earth or Mars moving around the Sun.

The Rigveda, a religious book from India created in about 1500 BC, refers to astronomy.

Ursa Major

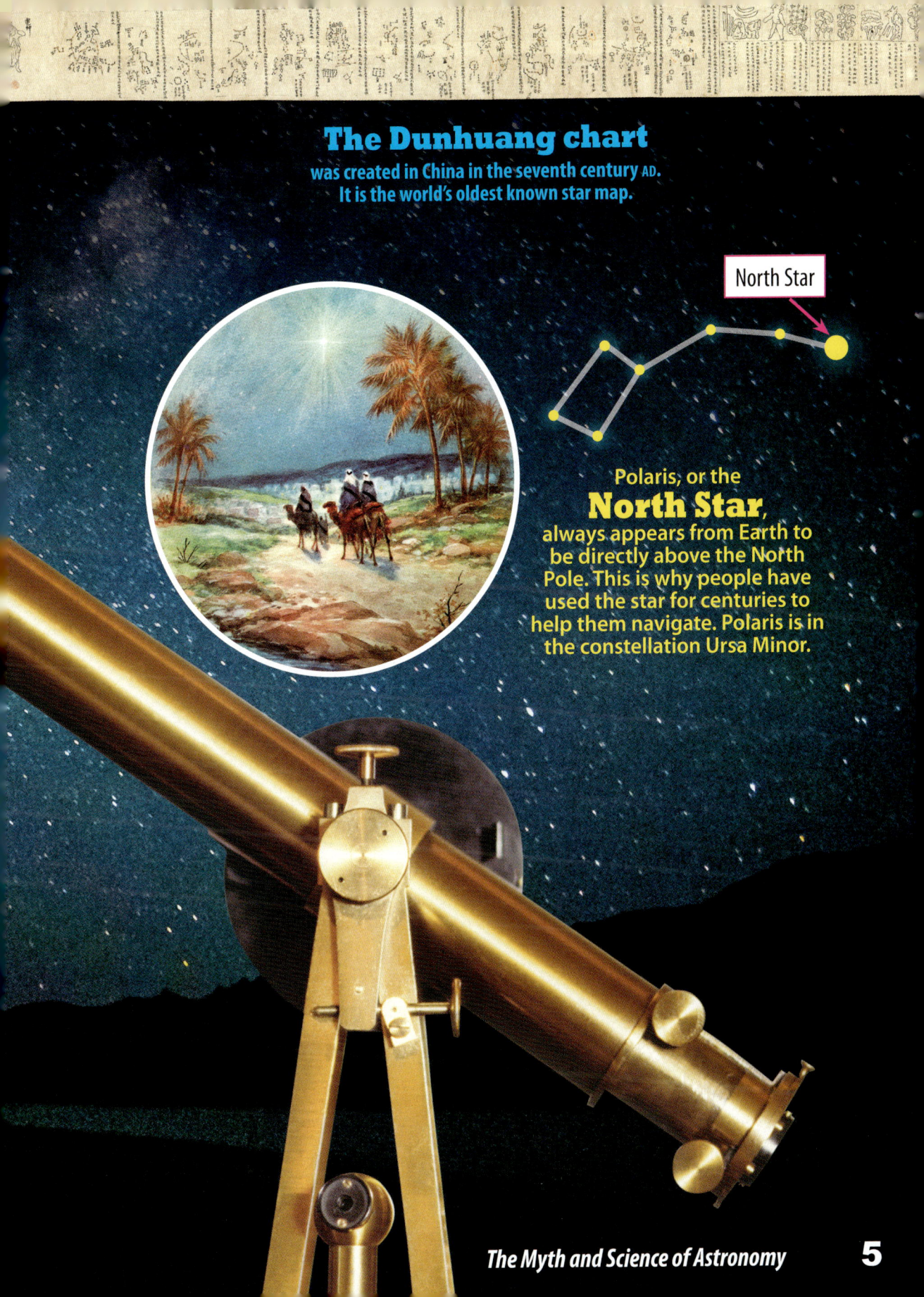

The Dunhuang chart
was created in China in the seventh century AD. It is the world's oldest known star map.

North Star

Polaris, or the
North Star,
always appears from Earth to be directly above the North Pole. This is why people have used the star for centuries to help them navigate. Polaris is in the constellation Ursa Minor.

The Myth and Science of Astronomy

Storytelling

Around the world, constellations have become part of folklore, or traditional customs, stories, and art. Throughout history, people have tried to explain the patterns they saw in the night sky. They created imaginary figures using the stars in the sky, as in a game of connect the dots. Some constellations were named after characters in ancient legends. Other constellations were named after animals. People also created stories about the figures in the night sky.

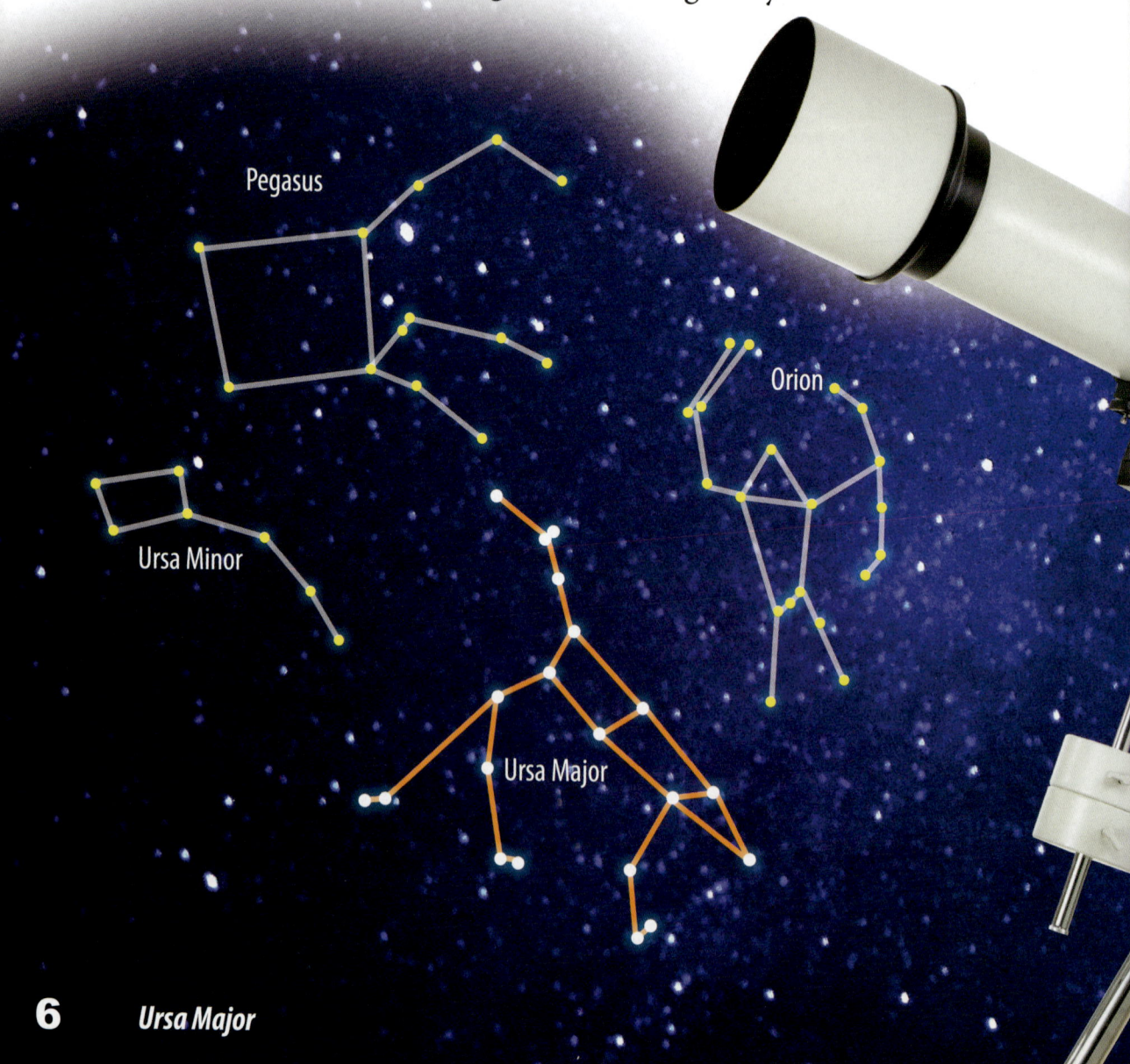

Pegasus

Orion

Ursa Minor

Ursa Major

Some of the best-known constellations are seen in the Northern Hemisphere. They include Hercules, Cygnus, Pegasus, Andromeda, Orion, and Ursa Major. The Ursa Major and Ursa Minor constellations get their names from ancient Greek storytelling.

Cygnus the Swan

Hercules

Andromeda

The Myth and Science of Astronomy

Ursa Major the Great Bear

Many constellations are named after heroes. The heroes appear in stories about **supernatural** creatures and events. A collection of these stories is called mythology.

Who Was Ursa Major?

Ursa Major appears in legends of the ancient Greeks. The name *Ursa Major* means "Great Bear" in Latin. This was the language of the ancient Romans. Rome took control of Greece in the 100s BC, and the Romans adopted many Greek gods and stories.

In one story, Zeus, the ruler of the gods, fell in love with a beautiful **nymph** named Callisto. Zeus and Callisto had a child. They named him Arcas. Zeus's wife, Hera, became very jealous. She turned Callisto into a bear.

> In works of art, Zeus often appears as a tall, bearded wise man.

The Story of Ursa Major

Many years later, Arcas was walking in the woods. Callisto the bear saw her son and ran to him. However, Arcas did not recognize her. Arcas was afraid the bear would attack him, and he took out his spear. Looking down from Mount Olympus, the home of the gods, Zeus saw what was about to happen. He sent down a whirlwind to sweep up Arcas and Callisto. Then, he placed both of them in the sky so they could be safe forever. Callisto became Ursa Major, and Arcas became the constellation *Ursa Minor*, or "Little Bear."

> According to one version of the Greek myth, Arcas served as king of Arcadia, a mountainous region named after him. He met Callisto while out hunting with his dogs.

The Myth and Science of Astronomy

The Origins of Ursa Major

Many of the world's different cultures have a story about Ursa Major. American Indians see the constellation as a "Great Bear." Some Arab cultures in the Middle East view the stars as a coffin with mourners. In old German stories, Ursa Major is called the *Grosse Wagen*, which means "big wagon" in German. The ancient Chinese referred to the constellation as a basket. In Mongolia, the seven brightest stars in the Ursa Major constellation are known as the Seven Gods.

From the 1820s until 1861, Ursa Major helped enslaved African Americans in the southern United States escape to free states in the North and to Canada. The slaves hid during the day and moved by night along what was called the Underground Railroad. This was a network of secret routes and safe stopping places. As they traveled, slaves used the stars Dubhe and Merak in Ursa Major, which point north, to find their way to freedom.

In an 18th-century painting from Korea, the seven brightest stars of Ursa Major appear as seven versions of the spiritual leader named Buddha.

The Stars of Ursa Major

The Big Dipper The seven brightest stars in Ursa Major form a shape called the Big Dipper. This cup with a long handle is one of the best-known shapes in the sky. It is also known as the Plough, or Plow, which is a tool that turns over soil.

Epsilon Ursae Majoris This is the brightest star in the constellation. It is also known as Alioth. It is the star in the tail of the bear closest to the body. Alioth is more than 100 times brighter than the Sun.

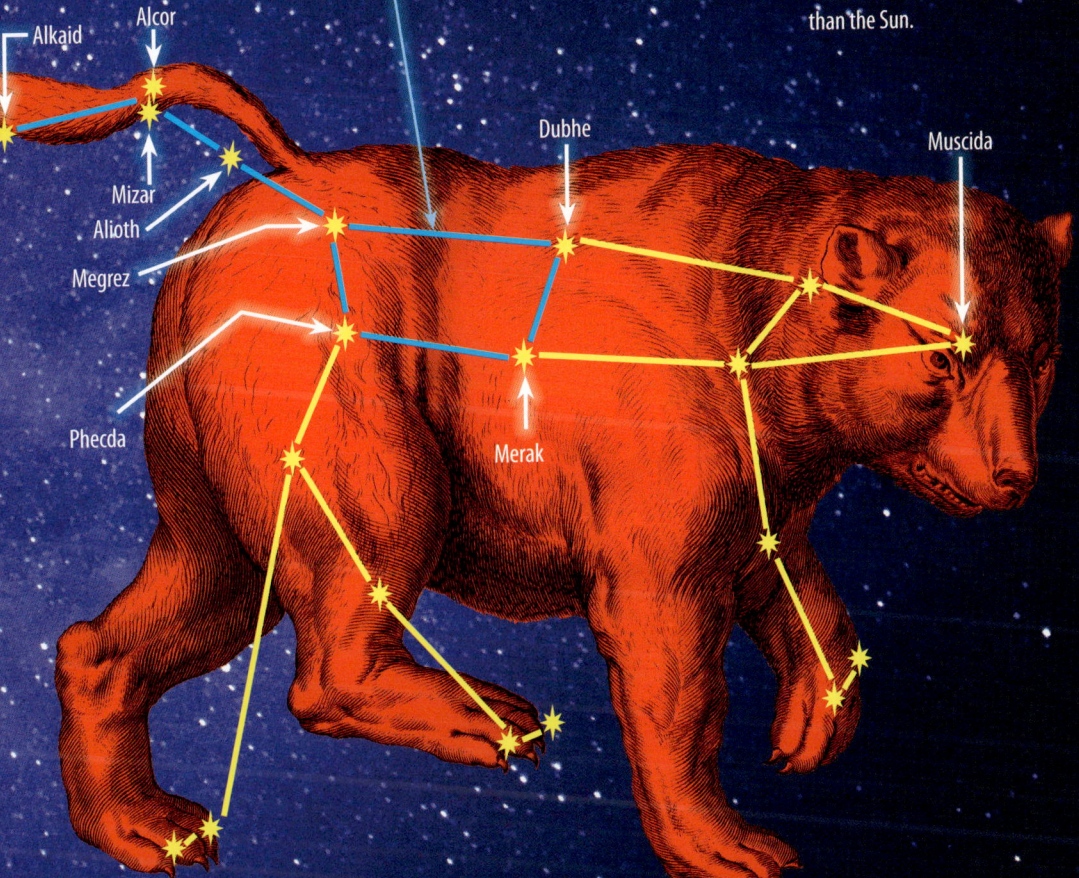

Alkaid
Alcor
Mizar
Alioth
Megrez
Phecda
Dubhe
Merak
Muscida

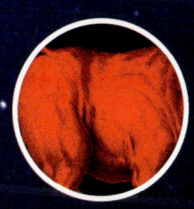

Alpha Ursae Majoris This is Ursa Major's second brightest star. It is also called *Dubhe*, or "the bear" in Arabic. Dubhe is a red giant, a star that is becoming bigger and cooler, has a red color, and will eventually explode.

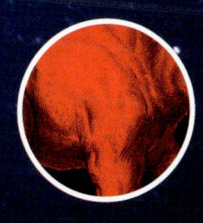

Eta Ursae Majoris This star, also known as Alkaid or Benetnash, is at the end of the Big Dipper. It is the third brightest star in Ursa Major.

Beta Ursae Majoris This star is also known as Merak. It is about 60 times brighter than the Sun.

The Myth and Science of Astronomy

Astronomy through History

Akkadian Tablet

Map Based on Ptolemy's Research

AD 150
Claudius Ptolemy of Egypt names 48 constellations.

2500 BC
In Mesopotamia, the Akkadian civilization compiles the earliest known astronomy records.

130 BC
The Greek astronomer Hipparchus uses various tools to study the positions of stars. He creates the first accurate star map of more than 850 of the brightest stars.

350 BC
The Chinese astronomer Shi Shen creates a catalog of 800 stars.

3000 BC
The Sumerians, in the Middle East region known as Mesopotamia, make lists of the brightest stars and name the constellations in the zodiac for the first time.

Hipparchus

12 *Ursa Major*

1609
Johannes Kepler

German astronomer Johannes Kepler publishes his laws about the motion of the planets. This is the first mathematical explanation that Earth revolves around the Sun.

1922

The International Astronomical Union names 88 official constellations. Of these, 36 constellations are in the northern sky, and 52 are in the southern sky.

1834

William Herschel's map of the sky defines the size and shape of the **Milky Way**, where Earth is located.

William Herschel

1990

The Hubble Space Telescope is launched.

Hubble Telescope

2018

The James Webb Space Telescope is scheduled for launch. More powerful than Hubble, it will search for galaxies not yet seen by humans.

The Myth and Science of Astronomy

Ursa Major over Time

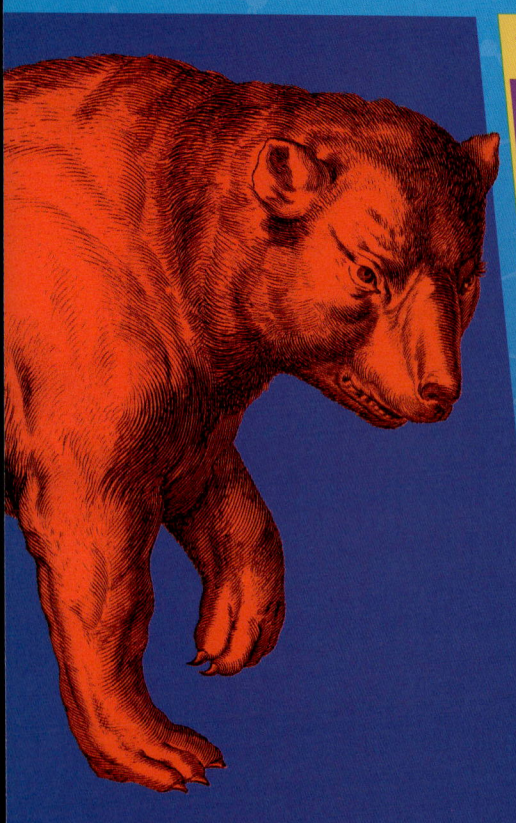

Astronomers have studied the Ursa Major constellation for centuries. In recent times, there have been some important scientific discoveries related to the Ursa Major constellation. They include finding galaxies and planets that earlier scientists did not know about.

1774 Discovery of Bode's Galaxy

Johann Elert Bode of Germany discovered a large **spiral galaxy** in Ursa Major in 1774. First called Messier 81 after the French astronomer Charles Messier, it was later named after Bode. Bode's Galaxy is closer to Earth than many other galaxies and is very bright. A **supernova** was discovered in the galaxy in 1993.

1781 The Owl Nebula in Ursa Major

French astronomer Pierre Mechain discovered the Owl **Nebula** in Ursa Major in 1781. As seen through a large telescope, the nebula has a shape similar to an owl's eyes. The nebula, which formed about 8,000 years ago, is 2,600 **light-years** away from Earth.

1781 The Pinwheel Galaxy Is Seen

Mechain discovered the Pinwheel Galaxy in Ursa Major in 1781. Messier later added it to the final version of his catalog. This catalog described more than 100 stars and other objects in space. The Pinwheel Galaxy is a large spiral galaxy that is almost twice the size of the Milky Way.

14 *Ursa Major*

1857 First Photograph of a Double Star

Zeta Ursae Majoris is a **binary star system** in the Big Dipper's handle. It also called Mizar. In 1857, U.S. astronomer George P. Bond and others photographed Mizar. It was the first double star ever captured on film.

1863 A Star Called Winnecke 4

Messier first saw and cataloged a star in Ursa Major now called Winnecke 4 in 1764. In 1863, Friedrich August Theodor Winnecke of Germany learned more about the star. It was later named after him. Winnecke 4 is about 510 light-years from Earth.

1996 Planets around a Sun-like Star

In 1996, astronomers discovered a large planet **orbiting** 47 Ursae Majoris, a star in Ursa Major. The planet is about twice the size of Jupiter. Two more planets orbiting 47 Ursae Majoris were discovered in 2002 and 2010. The 47 Ursae Majoris star, 46 light-years from Earth, is similar in size to the Sun.

The Myth and Science of Astronomy

Mapping Planetariums

At a planetarium, visitors can see exhibits about space and images of the night sky. A large room in the planetarium, often called a sky theater, has a dome-shaped ceiling. Pictures of objects in space are shown on the ceiling, while viewers listen to information about those objects. Some planetariums have telescopes for visitors to see the night sky for themselves. This map shows where some of the best-known planetariums in the United States can be found.

Washington

Oregon

Montana

Idaho

Wyoming

Nevada

Utah

Gates Planetarium, Denver, Colorado

Colorado

California

Arizona

New Mexico

Samuel Oschin Planetarium, Los Angeles, California

Pacific Ocean

Morrison Planetarium, San Francisco, California
The Morrison Planetarium is a part of the California Academy of Sciences. It has shows about the night sky and objects in space. Scientists at other research locations give talks that are shown on video. They provide information about Earth, other planets, stars, and ways to explore space.

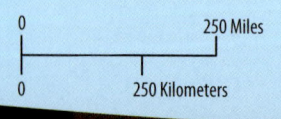

0 — 250 Miles
0 — 250 Kilometers

16   *Ursa Major*

Adler Planetarium, Chicago, Illinois
The Adler Planetarium is a leader in science education. The planetarium has theater programs, exhibits featuring historic telescopes, and special events. In the Grainger Sky Theater, visitors learn about the night sky as they seem to journey through space.

Hayden Planetarium, New York, New York

Strasenburgh Planetarium, Rochester, New York

Albert Einstein Planetarium, Washington, D.C.

Burke Baker Planetarium, Houston, Texas

Morehead Planetarium, Chapel Hill, North Carolina
The Morehead Planetarium and Science Center at the University of North Carolina is the largest full-dome planetarium in the southeastern United States. Its theater offers many different shows. Visitors can also take part in live science demonstrations in the Science Stage. The planetarium has summer science camps and an after-school club for students.

The Myth and Science of Astronomy

Careers in Astronomy

ASTRONOMERS often study for many years to prepare for their careers. Many future astronomers take classes in mathematics, physics, and other types of science during high school. At college, they often study physics, mathematics, engineering, and computer science. After graduating, many astronomers go on to receive a master's or doctor's degree. Astronomers often spend many years doing research to try to answer questions about objects in space.

SOFTWARE ENGINEERS design computer programs for astronomers. These programs are used to study and analyze information about stars and other objects in space. Software engineers usually have a master's or doctor's degree in computer science, as well as training in other related fields. These engineers must stay informed about the latest astronomy research.

EDUCATORS teach classes and lead educational activities about astronomy at science museums. They also create programs to inform the public about astronomy and space. People who want to become educators need a strong interest in astronomy and should be comfortable with public speaking. They should study math, science, and computers in high school and college.

Sky Facts

Many Stars

In 2005, the Hubble Space Telescope found 197 large star clusters in the center of the Cigar Galaxy in Ursa Major. Clusters are stars kept close together by gravity, a force that pulls objects toward one another.

Pointing North

The stars Merak and Dubhe in Ursa Major are often called the pointers because together they point to the North Star.

GREAT BEAR PLANETS

The Ursa Major constellation has 13 stars that are known to have planets.

Astronomy: Studying the Night Sky

Astronomy Q and A

1 **How many stars are in the Milky Way?**

Earth's Milky Way galaxy has between 200 billion and 400 billion stars. Some other galaxies are much bigger. The Andromeda Galaxy contains one trillion stars.

2 **How many stars can a person see at night without a telescope?**

A person can see about 3,000 stars at night without using a telescope. He or she needs to be far away from city lights on a clear night with no moon.

3 **What is a supergiant?**

Supergiants are the largest types of stars. They vary in size but can be thousands of times bigger than Earth's Sun. Supergiants are usually blue or red. Blue supergiants are the hottest.

4 **Why do stars shine?**

Stars are giant balls of glowing gas. This gas is so hot that a process called nuclear fusion takes place. In this process, two **atoms** come together to form a new atom. Fusion also produces huge amounts of energy that people see as light.

5 **Which constellation is the largest?**

Hydra is the constellation that covers the largest area of the sky. It is named after a snake with nine heads in Greek mythology. Hydra is seen in the Southern Hemisphere.

Create Your Own Star Catalog

You can create your own star catalog. This is a fun way to learn about constellations that are visible where you live. This activity is for constellations in the Northern Hemisphere.

What You Need: Large spiral notebook, Pencil, Compass

1 Using the information in this book and online, find pictures of the constellations Ursa Major, Ursa Minor, Cassiopeia, Gemini, Taurus, and Orion. Draw or print and paste these constellations in your notebook to use later as a guide.

2 On each of 12 pages, across the top of the page, write the names of the six constellations. Along the left-hand margin, write *Date* on the first line, *Time* on the second line, and *Direction* on the third line.

3 You are ready to begin. On the first of the 12 pages, record the date and time in your notebook. Locate as many of the six constellations as you can in the night sky.

4 For each one, using the compass to guide you, record whether you need to look toward the east, west, north or south to see the constellation. Remember, you may not be able to see all the constellations year round.

5 Repeat steps 3 and 4 once a month for the next 11 months. At the end of a year, you will have created your own star catalog. It will tell you the months of the year when each constellation is visible in your area. The *Direction* information will show how the positions of some constellations in the sky change during a year.

The Myth and Science of Astronomy

Know Your Stars Quiz

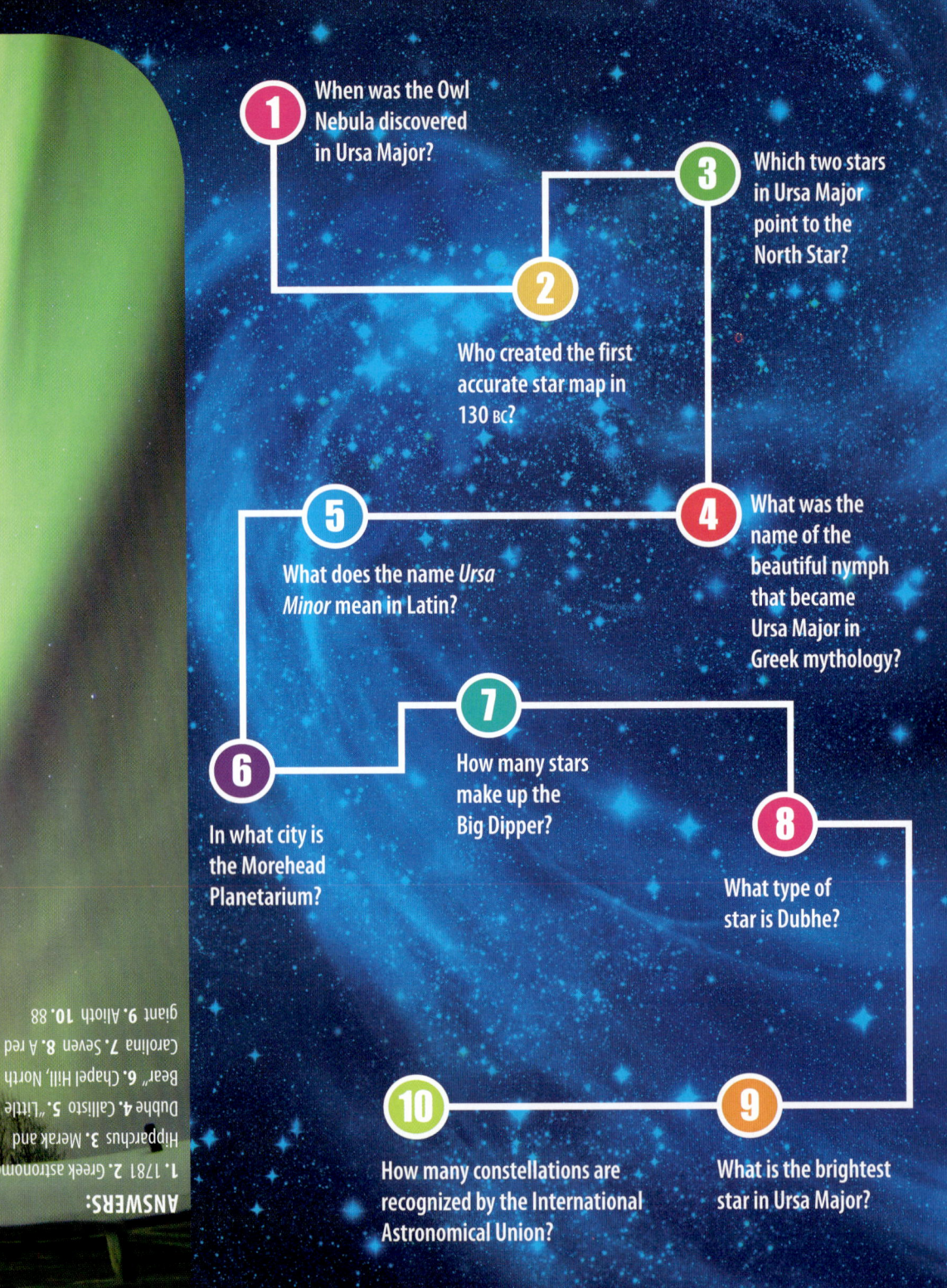

1 When was the Owl Nebula discovered in Ursa Major?

2 Who created the first accurate star map in 130 BC?

3 Which two stars in Ursa Major point to the North Star?

4 What was the name of the beautiful nymph that became Ursa Major in Greek mythology?

5 What does the name *Ursa Minor* mean in Latin?

6 In what city is the Morehead Planetarium?

7 How many stars make up the Big Dipper?

8 What type of star is Dubhe?

9 What is the brightest star in Ursa Major?

10 How many constellations are recognized by the International Astronomical Union?

ANSWERS: 1. 1781 2. Greek astronomer Hipparchus 3. Merak and Dubhe 4. Callisto 5. "Little Bear" 6. Chapel Hill, North Carolina 7. Seven 8. A red giant 9. Alioth 10. 88

Ursa Major

Key Words

atoms: the smallest units of a substance that can exist by themselves

binary star system: two stars that orbit a common center of gravity, the force that pulls objects toward one another

civilizations: groups of people who live in the same area and share beliefs and a way of life

comets: large balls of ice and rock in space that travel around the Sun

galaxies: groups of millions or billions of stars, as well as the dust and gas around them

hemisphere: one half of a sphere such as Earth

light-years: distances that light travels in one year

Milky Way: the galaxy that includes Earth and its solar system and appears as a white band of stars in the night sky

nebula: a large cloud of dust and gases in space

nymph: a female spirit of the natural world that lives in water, forests, and mountains

orbiting: traveling around an object in a curved path

spiral galaxy: a galaxy that has long arms curving around the center

supernatural: related to gods, spirits, or events that cannot be explained by science

supernova: a very large explosion that occurs when a huge star dies, or burns out

telescopes: devices used to detect and observe distant objects

Index

Alioth 11, 22
Arcas 8, 9

Big Dipper 11, 15, 22
Bode's Galaxy 14

Callisto 8, 9, 22

Dubhe 10, 11, 19, 22

Merak 10, 11, 19
Messier, Charles 14, 15
Morehead Planetarium 17, 22

Owl Nebula 14, 22

Pinwheel Galaxy 14

Ursa Minor 5, 6, 7, 9, 21, 22

Winnecke 4 15

Zeus 8, 9

The Myth and Science of Astronomy

LIGHTB◆X

⊕ SUPPLEMENTARY RESOURCES

Click on the plus icon ⊕ found in the bottom left corner of each spread to open additional teacher resources.

- Download and print the book's quizzes and activities
- Access curriculum correlations
- Explore additional web applications that enhance the Lightbox experience

LIGHTBOX DIGITAL TITLES
Packed full of integrated media

VIDEOS

INTERACTIVE MAPS

WEBLINKS

SLIDESHOWS

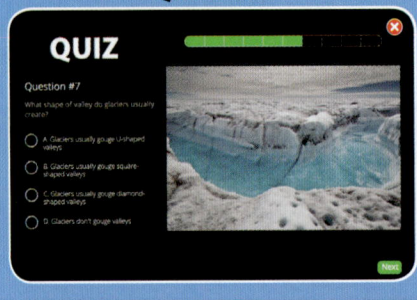

QUIZZES

OPTIMIZED FOR
✓ TABLETS
✓ WHITEBOARDS
✓ COMPUTERS
✓ AND MUCH MORE!

Published by Smartbook Media, Inc.
350 5th Avenue, 59th Floor
New York, NY 10118
Website: www.openlightbox.com

Copyright © 2016 Smartbook Media, Inc.
All rights reserved. No part of this publication may be reproduced, stored in a retrieval system, or transmitted in any form or by any means, electronic, mechanical, photocopying, recording, or otherwise, without the prior written permission of the publisher.

Library of Congress Cataloging-in-Publication Data
Rose, Simon, 1961- author.
    Ursa major / Simon Rose.
        pages cm. -- (The Myth and Science of Astronomy)
    Includes index.
    ISBN 978-1-5105-0022-8 (hard cover : alk. paper) --
    ISBN 978-1-5105-0270-5 (soft cover : alk. paper) --
    ISBN 978-1-5105-0023-5 (multi-user ebook)
    1. Constellations--Juvenile literature. 2. Astronomy--Juvenile literature. 3. Ursa Major--Juvenile literature. 4. Ursa Major--Legends--Juvenile literature. I. Title.
    QB802.R66 2016

523.8--dc23

2014041045

Printed in Brainerd, Minnesota, United States
1 2 3 4 5 6 7 8 9 19 18 17 16 15

052015
051715

Project Coordinator Aaron Carr
Art Director Terry Paulhus

Note: Constellations shown on pages 6 and 7 are n necessarily in their actual positions in the night sk

Photo Credits
Every reasonable effort has been made to trace ownership and to obtain permission to reprint copyright material. The publisher would be pleased to have any errors or omissions brought to its attention so that they may be corrected in subsequent printings.

The publisher acknowledges Getty Images as its primary photo supplier for this title.

24 *Ursa Major*